REMINGTON

REMINGTON

Jessica Hodge

SATURN BOOKS

This edition published 1997 by Saturn
Books, Kiln House, 210 New Kings
Road, London SW6 4NZ.

ISBN 1 86222 005 0

Printed in Singapore

CONTENTS

INTRODUCTION

The art of the American West, so convincingly and dramatically encapsulated in the work of Frederic Remington, took its inspiration from an irresistible tide of westward expansion, which reached its peak in the 1840s with the discovery of gold in California. The Louisiana Purchase in 1803 opened up a vast central area for exploration and settlement, establishing the western boundaries of the United States of America in present-day Colorado and Wyoming, and in the next 50 years the American people steadily pushed the frontier westward. The Texas republic was annexed in 1845; in 1846 the northwest Pacific coast was opened up with the acquisition of the territory of Oregon; and in 1848 the vast southwestern Pacific area was ceded by Mexico as the spoils of war. In 1849 alone, 80,000 people poured into California.

While it was possible to get to the Pacific coast by ship round Cape Horn, or by the dangerous, difficult shortcut across the Isthmus of Panama, by far the most popular route was across the plains by covered wagon. In the wake of the gold prospectors came commercial mining operations; then the farmers and ranchers moved in to establish a more permanent economy; and as miners, cowmen, and ranchers settled, they came face-to-face with the indigenous population, the Native Americans, whose determined and sustained resistance lasted well into the 1880s.

Even the earliest exploratory expeditions

LEFT: Remington (first row extreme right), was a rusher in Yale's 1879 football team.

RIGHT: A cartoon of Remington and his wife, Eva.

occasionally included artists, whose pictorial records are of immense historic value, even if not, on the whole, of any artistic significance. The first artist of real stature to go west was George Catlin, who, recognizing that the Native American way of life was doomed, travelled all over the West in the 1830s and visited 48 tribes, living with them, learning their languages, and familiarizing himself with their customs and way of life. Catlin was something of an exception, however, with his elegiac celebration of Native American mores; the more common artistic message of the 1830s and 1840s was one of triumphal progress. America was the country of the future, and expansion was seen as a prerequisite to the infant nation's destiny as an international leader.

Perhaps the greatest achievement of Frederic Remington was to combine, in one forceful body of work, this self-confident, celebratory mood with Catlin's romantic sense of a fast vanishing culture. For Remington, however, the transitory quality he perceived applied quite as much to the cowboy as to the "Indian." The land mass that had been opened up with such astonishing speed was settled and tamed almost as rapidly; artists such as Remington, and his almost-contemporary Charles Russell, took it upon themselves to record a frontier way of life that was no sooner established than, by its very nature, it was threatened.

Writing in 1905, at the height of his career, Remington recalled his early motivation:

"I saw men all ready (sic) swarming into the land. I knew the derby hat, the smoking chimneys, the cord binders, and the thirty-day notes were upon us in a restless surge. I knew the wild riders and the vacant land were about to vanish forever . . . and the more I considered the subject, the bigger the forever loomed. Without knowing exactly how to do it, I began to try to record some facts around me, and the more I looked the more the panorama unfolded . . . I saw the living, breathing end of three American centuries of smoke and dust and sweat."

Over a period of almost 30 years, Remington recorded this frontier world not only in nearly 3,000 paintings and drawings, but also in 25 bronze sculptures, nine books, a play, and countless magazine articles. His energy was prodigious, and his ability to move from medium to medium was regarded as extraordinary, even in an age that prized ecleticism.

Remington's first success was as an illustrator rather than as an artist, a distinction about which he

was to remain sensitive throughout his career. Illustration did not become part of the academic program in schools until the 1890s, and illustrators generally had less formal education than trained artists, acquiring their skills on the job and tending to work within a fairly limited range of subject matter. They relied for their success as much on their knowledge of customs, costumes, and accessories as on their abilities as draftsmen. While artists such as Thomas Eakins and James McNeill Whistler chose to expose themselves to the stimulus of European art by visiting that decadent continent, such experience was deemed irrelevant to the illustrator, and Remington showed little enthusiasm for leaving his native shores. But he was certainly not without ambition, as clear in the wildly energetic, if equally opportunistic, letter he wrote at the age of 17 to his aunt:

"I want a situation as son-in-law to a first class family — no objection to going a few miles into the country. I want an English walking jacket — fur collar and cuffs. I want L'Art for a year. I want de Neuville's last autotype. I want some half hundred books. I want

RIGHT: Remington painting *The French Trapper.*

LEFT: Remington's home in New Rochelle, New York, where he moved in 1892.

BELOW: *Giving the Butt,* Remington's first signed illustration for *Harpers Weekly.*

about a million Henry Clay cigars. I want a smoking set — not the common kind — but the uncommon kind. I want a board bill paid in advance for four weeks at Fire Island. Oh laws I want everything — everything and nothing at all. Guess I wouldn't buy anything for such a feller as I am."

It galled him immensely that during his lifetime his concern with portraying realistically the world he came to know so well led critics to continue to regard him simply as an illustrator. The commitment to realism that in fact links Remington with a powerful and enduring trend in American art caused him to be dismissed by his contemporaries, for much of his career, as a chronicler rather than an artist. Today his paintings command high prices among American collectors, although still not in Europe. His early patrons were not "serious" collectors, however, but individuals such as Amon Carter and Sid Richardson, both legendary Texan oilmen, who valued Remington's work for its local and narrative value, rather than its artistic quality.

More than any other artist, Remington focused on the social history of the West; he saw it from the beginning as a process of settlement carried on by a series of "types," such as a "Texan cowboy," a "French Canadian trapper," a "Mexican vacquero," and a "puncher." His great advantage was that he was present at, and able to record for a voracious public back east, the final stages of an epic saga. The last great buffalo slaughter occurred on the northern plains in 1881, the year that he first travelled west; he was commissioned to record the capture of the Apache chief Geronimo; he was invited to Montana to observe the U.S. Army's handling of the last great Sioux uprising of 1890, during which Sitting Bull was killed. And the vast growth of the magazine and newspaper industry during the last quarter of the 19th century gave him a ready market for the dramatic, immediate images that he was moved to create.

Frederic Sackrider Remington was born on October 1, 1861, to a well-to-do family in Canton, New York, a small town some 25 miles from the Canadian border. His father, Seth Pierre Remington, was the proprietor of a local newspaper who responded to the

LEFT: Remington in later life, with his canoe at his island retreat, Ingleneuk, on the St. Lawrence river.

ABOVE: Frederic Remington at his easel.

Congressional call to arms in the year of his only child's birth, and distinguished himself as a Union cavalry officer in the Civil War. In 1873 Seth was made customs' collector at the port of Ogdensburg, a larger town than Canton, about 12 miles away on the St. Lawrence River, in an area to which the young Frederic remained attached throughout his life.

Because of his own experience, and the opportunities offered by military service, Seth wanted his son to consider the military as a career. Frederic was accordingly sent first to the Vermont Episcopal Institute in Burlington, and then, in 1874, to the Highland Military Academy in Worcester, Massachusetts. A large, restless, physically active child, the young Remington showed no particular interest in or aptitude for academic studies and resisted military discipline, but he did excel at drawing, a desirable talent for a soldier as a means of conveying essential strategic information. One of the earliest sketches that survives from this period shows

the 15-year-old Remington's reaction to the defeat of Colonel Custer's forces at the Battle of Little Big Horn. Fifteen years later, he portrayed the scene in a strikingly similar fashion in his dramatic painting *The Last Stand* (1890)

By the time that Remington graduated from Highland in 1878, he had made up his mind to pursue an artistic career, and enrolled in the School of Fine Arts at Yale University, the first university-level professional art school in the country. The school was under the direction of John Ferguson Weir, an accomplished, European-trained artist known for his dramatic portrayals of heavy industry, and instruction in drawing followed the classic precept of working only from plaster casts. Again Remington found the discipline irksome, and in later life liked to portray himself as self-taught, maintaining that he never took anyone's advice. He advised an aspiring young artist: "Study good pictures and above all draw — draw — draw — and always from nature."

More to Remington's taste at Yale was the university's sporting arena, and he took to both boxing and football with gusto. In 1880, however, after he had completed rather less than two years of study, his father died, leaving Remington half his estate when he attained the age of 21. Until then he needed to earn a living, and experimented fitfully with a number of jobs but settled on none, despite the incentive of falling in love with a neighbour, Eva Caten, whose father insisted that Remington should prove himself in a career before there could be any question of marriage. Remington's uncle found him a more challenging post with the State Insurance Department in Albany, starting in October 1881, but first Remington was determined to fulfil his ambition to explore Montana and Wyoming, in the hope of making his fortune and returning to Eva a made man.

In the raw, volatile, macho atmosphere of the West, Remington found just the stimulus that his energetic temperament and enquiring mind needed. He made a considerable number of sketches, one of which he succeeded in selling to the influential magazine *Harper's Weekly* back in New York. *Harper's* was impressed by the freshness and realism of his rendering of Arizona cowboys roused by a scout, but not by its technical quality, and the sketch was redrawn by a staff artist before publication.

In October 1882, after a year of worthy toil, Remington came into his inheritance and decided to invest the whole sum, $9,000, in a sheep farm in Kansas. The year he spent here during the heyday of the cattlemen, the only significant period he spent on the plains, provided the firsthand information on which much of his later work was based. The "long drives" of cattle began in Texas, moved north along trails such as the Chisholm and the Shawnee, and terminated in railroad towns such as Abilene and Kansas City. The combined herds, numbering between 2,000 and 5,000 head of cattle, were driven by cowpunchers or cowboys, an impressive sight with their 40-pound saddles, 20-foot lariats, six revolvers, chaps, and sombreros. Theirs was both a dangerous and a dull existence; it was the former that attracted Remington.

Ranching, however, proved an unattractive proposition. Remington sold the ranch at a loss in spring 1884 and took an extended sketching trip through the Southwest. On his return to Kansas City, he invested as a sleeping partner in a saloon, bought a house, and returned east intent on persuading Eva to marry him. By sheer force of personality he convinced both Eva and her father that there was a fortune to be made in the West, but the early days of the marriage were fairly disastrous. Kansas City was a rugged place for a young, gently bred girl, and few in the area were interested in Frederic's art. The saloon proved a bad investment and after a few months of increasing poverty, Eva returned east to her parents. Remington again travelled southwest, this time to Arizona, where Geronimo and the Apaches were known to be active, to the San Carlos Reservation, set aside for the resettlement of the Apaches, and then north into Indian Territory and the Comanche reservation.

BELOW: *Water Lilies* – a sample from Remington's photo album, and possibly a study for one of his paintings

RIGHT: *Marching in the Desert* – one of Remington's illustrations for *The Century* magazine, published in April 1889.

Remington is pictured in the center wearing the sun helmet, riding with the U.S. (Negro) Cavalry regiment.

Returning in fall 1885 with a portfolio jammed with sketches, Remington made the critical decision to take his work back east and seek a career as an illustrator in New York. The time was right; magazines such as *Harper's Weekly*, *Scribner's*, and *The Century Illustrated Monthly Magazine* were all catering to a insatiable public demand for information about the West. Within a few weeks, Remington had sold two drawings to the owner of *Harper's*, Henry Harper himself, and his career was launched. He was reunited with Eva and the couple settled in a Brooklyn apartment. Although confident of his own abilities, Remington recognized that, compared with other published artists, he lacked technical ability, and in March 1886 he enrolled at the Art Students League, a loosely organized school, where well-known painters both taught and attended classes.

In summer 1886 Remington again headed southwest, this time, however, with a commission from *Harper's Weekly* to follow and report on the Indian wars, especially the campaign being waged by General Nelson Miles against Geronimo. He returned not only with another portfolio full of drawings, but also with two new and valuable friends. One of these was General Miles himself, the other was Lieutenant Powhattan Clarke, with whom Remington maintained a regular correspondence until Clarke's death in 1893. Clarke proved a rich source of information about the

details of army life in the Southwest. *Harper's* was so impressed with Remington's illustrations that they were published weekly, and Remington also landed a major contract with *Century Magazine* to illustrate Theodore Roosevelt's series of stories, "Ranch Life and the Hunting Trail." He got on well with Roosevelt, who shared with him a historian's interest in the heroic, and who remained one of his principal supporters throughout his life. Among the 83 illustrations that he produced for the project were several grisaille (black-and-white) paintings, the best of which is *An Episode in the Opening Up of a Cattle Country* (1887).

It was in the early 1880s, just as he was becoming established as an illustrator, that Remington first set his heart on becoming a painter, but the first flood of drawing commissions kept him immensely busy, and it was only in 1887 that he felt financially secure enough to turn seriously to painting. Unlike many of his contemporaries, subject matter was always his primary concern, whether as an artist or an illustrator. During a period when foreign subjects as well as foreign styles were enormously popular, Remington from the outset devoted himself solely to American subject matter, and largely specialized in one particular aspect of his chosen area, the West. Even among those artists who shared Remington's commitment to subject, few embraced strictly American themes with

his degree of enthusiasm. The art world of the time was dominated by cosmopolitan painters such as Whistler, George Inness, and Thomas W. Dewing, who were principally preoccupied with the formal qualities of their art — line, color, and design — and sought subjects that enabled them to transcend external appearance and suggest moods and emotions. Remington, on the contrary, expressed his philosophy thus: "I stand for the proposition of 'subjects' painting something worthwhile as against painting nothing merely paint."

The first oil painting to be accorded the kind of recognition that Remington craved was Return of the Blackfoot War Party (1887), which was accepted for the annual National Academy of Design show in 1888

and won two prizes. In the course of the following year, Remington's income doubled. In 1889 he entered a large oil, Last Lull in the Fight, to the American jury selecting work for the 1889 Paris International Exposition, and had the satisfaction of winning a second-place medal. This in turn encouraged him to explore other large subjects for purposes of exhibition, and in 1889 he created what is undoubtedly one of his greatest paintings, A Dash for the Timber. A dramatic narrative work showing eight cowboys riding for the shelter of the woods pursued by a hostile band of Indians, it was based on Remington's journal notes and demonstrated his close study of horses and riders in motion. When exhibited at the National Academy of Design, the painting was

LEFT: Photograph taken in the 1870s of women from the Sioux tribe in Dakota working on staked down buffalo skins. Buffalo meat is drying on poles in the background.

ABOVE: *Buying Polo Ponies in the West* from a painting by Remington published in *The Illustrated Sporting and Dramatic News* of 14 May 1910.

praised by the New York Times critic as "rendering with unusual truth effects of strong sunlight," but the *New York Herald* came closer to Remington's purpose: "the drawing is true and strong, the figures of men and horses are in fine action, tearing along at full gallop, the sunshine effect is realistic and the color is good."

Already the most respected illustrator in America, Remington now seemed to be earning similar recognition for his easel work. Flown with success, he purchased a substantial estate at New Rochelle, where he and Eva settled to a comfortable life of social visits and annual vacations on the St. Lawrence or in the Adirondacks, where Remington hunted and fished interminably. He also made at least one trip a year west, now laden with commissions, and sometimes also to Canada or Mexico. By 1890 he was painting simultaneously for exhibition and illustration, and in June 1891 he was elected an associate of the National Academy of Design, the second-highest honor his artist peers could bestow. In a phenomenal burst of energy, he produced a string of formidable paintings, including *An Indian Trapper*

ABOVE: The Last Lull in the Fight.

RIGHT: *The Apache War* Remington's first signed cover for *Harpers Weekly*, dated 9 January 1886.

(1889), *Arrival of a Courier* (1890), which includes the dashing figure of his friend Clarke, *The Cavalryman's Breakfast on the Plains* (1890), and *The Last Stand*.

Exhibiting paintings put greater pressure on Remington to move beyond considerations simply of subject matter and to tackle such subtle aspects of painting as expression, color harmonies, paint quality, and the structure of the painting itself. Probably anticipating his imminent election to the highest level the National Academy of Design could bestow, that of Academician, Remington decided in 1892 to accompany his old friend from Yale, Poultney Bigelow, on a visit to Europe, both for the sake of his artistic development and as an opportunity to see European military men and arms at close range. The two men visited Germany and Russia, and apparently planned a canoe trip down the Volga River, but Bigelow, son of the American ambassador to Germany, was suspected by the Russians of spying, and the two men were unceremoniously ejected from the country. Returning to the United States via Paris and London, Remington wrote to Clarke: "I hate Europe and nothing but due necessity will ever draw me there again."

Remington's sole completed self-portrait dates from about this time, and may well have been painted with a view to submission to the National Academy of Design, which required a full member to submit either

HARPER'S WEEKLY.

JOURNAL OF CIVILIZATION.

Vol. XXX.—No. 1516.
Copyright, 1886, by Harper & Brothers.

NEW YORK, SATURDAY, JANUARY 9, 1886.

TEN CENTS A COPY.
$4.00 PER YEAR, IN ADVANCE.

THE APACHE WAR—INDIAN SCOUTS ON GERONIMO'S TRAIL.—Drawn by Frederic Remington.—[See Page 23.]

a self-portrait or a portrait of himself by another artist. *Self Portrait on a Horse* (c.1890) was submitted, but Remington, with dangerous complacency, then failed to submit another major work for exhibition for several years, and the academy never did accord him the status of full Academician. In 1899 he made one last concerted effort when he submitted *Missing* (1899), but this static image is not Remington at his best, and the academy remained unresponsive.

Remington's failure to achieve full membership in the academy reflects an ambivalence toward the need for critical acceptance by the fine-art world that caused him to miss another major opportunity in 1893, when the World's Fair Columbian Exposition was staged in Chicago. The fair was America's response to the Paris fair of 1889, which was symbolized by the Eiffel Tower, and thus staked the country's claim to be considered a cultural leader among nations. The art catalog of the exposition is a who's who of contemporary American art, but Remington, failing to recognize the significance of the occasion, did not submit a single oil painting. In fact he did very little painting at this time and concentrated rather on articles for periodicals, culminating in his first book, *Pony Tracks*, which was published in 1895.

A period of depression and inactivity, provoked by what Remington perceived as the failure of the art world to accord him due recognition, ended in 1895, when he began experimenting with clay sculpture. As in his painting, Remington's prime interest was his subject matter. The first piece he created, *Bronco Buster* (1895), was derived from his own drawings

ABOVE: *The Wounded Bunkie*, bronze 20¾in high.

RIGHT: Buffalo slaughtered by white hunters in Montana, 1882.

and paintings of horse and rider. A brilliant composition, quite unlike anything produced before in the medium, it has since been hailed as an icon of the American West. Earlier bronzes had rarely shown a horse in motion, let alone in violent action; Remington's wildly lunging bronco demonstrated his ability to capture action as no other artist had, and proved immensely popular. His second work, *The Wounded Bunkie* (1896), combines a still more sophisticated composition. The entire sculpture is supported on just two horses' legs with a much greater sense of narrative drama. In subsequent work Remington moved away from the smooth surface and linear realism of these early pieces. Restored to full vigor by the challenge of a new medium, he spent many hours at the Roman Bronze Works in Brooklyn, learning the intricacies of bronze casting by the lost wax method, which had been all but superseded in the 18th and 19th centuries by the simpler sand-casting process. The first lost wax piece he created, *The Norther* (1900), demonstrates his skillful exploitation of the rich, textural effects that can be achieved through this process, while *The Cheyenne* (1901) combines the textural subtlety of *The Norther* with the sense of frozen motion that characterizes his earlier work.

In other areas Remington's career was proving less satisfactory. With the end of the Indian Wars, the

West was less attractive to him, as he wrote in 1900 to his wife: "Shall never come West again — It is all brick buildings — derby hats and blue overalls — it spoils my early illusions — and they are my capital." Instead he yearned for a real war, and in 1898 his opportunity came with the outbreak of hostilities between the United States and Spain. Remington, with commissions from both *Harper's* and the *New York Journal*, travelled with the invasion troops from Florida to Cuba in June 1898, but he was ill prepared and unfit, and found the brutal realities of open warfare more than he could stomach. He fell ill and had to return home, and the two large paintings he made on his return, *The Scream of Shrapnel at San Juan Hill* and *The Charge of the Rough Riders at San Juan Hill* (both 1898) are not among his most successful compositions. Depressed by this experience, Remington retired to Ingleneuk, the island in the St. Lawrence that he and Eva had bought in 1895. Never a lightweight, his weight soared to 300 pounds. A further blow came in 1899, when *Harper's* ended his contract after 15 years, but this was almost at once replaced by a more favorable contract with *Collier's: The National Weekly*, which required him to create paintings for reproduction and not just as

illustrations to accompany articles. Motivated and liberated by this open-ended agreement, Remington determined finally to overcome what he had long recognized as his inadequacy in the handling of color. As he wrote to one young artist:

"For ten years I've been trying to get color in my things and I still don't get it. Why, why, why can't I get it. The only reason I can find is that I have worked too long in black and white. I know fine color when I see it but I just don't get it and it's maddening. I'm going to if I only live long enough."

Surviving textbooks annotated by Remington at this time show how assiduously he applied himself to understanding the principles of color theory and using them in his work. One interesting development is the series of nocturnal paintings that he produced at about this time; their muted tones presented a narrower range of colors for a painter experimenting with color. By the time that he produced *The Questionable Companionship (The Parley)* in 1902, however, the development is clear. The cavalryman is not simply drawn, but is painted with a buildup of color, and the surrounding hills blend from greens in

the foreground to browns and purples in the distance, reflecting a new sensitivity to the painterly qualities of color. He began to work increasingly in the open air, following the Impressionist precept of setting up his easel in front of his motif, rather than working the subject up in the studio from notes and sketches. The result was a series of calm, atmospheric landscape studies of the area round Ingleneuk that were far removed from the clear line and frantic motion of the early Western paintings.

A one-man show in New York in 1906 was well-received, with one critic commenting approvingly that "he has worked out and away from his former hard and dry color and his pictures have a new softness and almost delicacy of color." As a result, Remington was offered an annual show. As if in final rejection of the role illustration had played in his work, he staged a series of massive bonfires in the next two years, each time after one of his shows, in which he destroyed much of the earlier work that he regarded as unworthy of his current stature. His 1908 show represented a breakthrough, in that it not only featured five landscape studies but also some of his

ABOVE: *Taking the Rope*, which shows professional white hunters stripping hide from buffalo.

RIGHT: *A Sergeant of U.S. Cavalry*, a drawing by Frederic Remington, taken from life in 1890.

very best Western paintings, including *Indians Simulating Buffalo*, *The Snow Trail*, *The Stampede*, and *With the Eye of the Mind*. The 1909 exhibition was the most highly praised of his entire career, drawing both critical acclaim and huge crowds. Much cheered, Remington noted in his diary on December 9, 1909:

"The art critics have all 'come down' I have belated but splendid notices from all the papers. They ungrudgingly give me a high place as a 'mere painter.' I have been on their trail a long while and they never surrendered while they had a leg to stand on. The 'Illustrator' phase has become background."

By the time the exhibition closed, eleven paintings had been sold for a total of over $5,000. The

Fredric Remington.

LEFT: Remington's interpretation of a freight wagon train and bull whackers on the Santa Fe Trail

LEFT: *The Indian or the Trooper* from a painting by Charles Schreyvogel.

RIGHT: *Texas Cowboy* painted by Remington around 1890.

Remingtons had enough to live on for a couple of years, and Remington was free to paint what he wanted. Two weeks later, he developed acute stomach pains. A doctor was called, acute appendicitis diagnosed, and an emergency operation carried out on the Remingtons' kitchen table. All seemed to have gone well, but the following day peritonitis developed, and within 24 hours Remington was dead.

By the time of his death, it was clear that he had both finally achieved success as an artist and that, despite his resistance to 'painting nothing merely paint,' this had been achieved through his adoption of many of the techniques of Impressionism. In a letter written at the end of his life, he referred to himself as a "plein air man by instinct," and yet the figure remained absolutely central in his art. It may seem tragically ironic that he should have died at the moment he did, but it is debatable whether any amount of late success would have provided an adequate counterweight to his early fame as an illustrator. In the event, his initial success and the reputation he established as the chronicler par excellence of the dying West, has continued to outweigh his late critical recognition as a painter.

Bronco Buster
Colored engraving
Peter Newark's Western Americana

Cowboy With Lariat
Peter Newark's Western Americana

U.S.Cavalry Officer in Campaign Dress
Peter Newark's Western Americana

RIDIN

Cowboy Riding the Line of the Barbed Wire Fence
Peter Newark's Western Americana

FREDERIC REMINGTON.

HE LINE OF THE WIRE FENCE.

The Sentinel 1889
Oil on canvas, 34 x 49 in.
Courtesy Sid Richardson Collection of Western Art, Fort Worth, TX

The Buffalo Hunt 1890
Oil on canvas, 34 x 49 in.
Buffalo Bill Historical Center, Cody, WY
Gift of William E. Weiss

The Thunder-Fighters Would Take their Bows and Arrows, Their Guns, Their Magic Drum 1892
Oil on wood panel, 30 x18 in.
Courtesy Sid Richardson Collection of Western Art, Fort Worth, TX

The Ambushed Picket 1886
Pencil, pen and ink and watercolor on paper, 9 x 11⅞ in.
Courtesy Sid Richardson Collection of Western Art, Fort Worth, Texas.

On the Trail 1889
Oil on canvas
Peter Newark's Western Americana

Mexican Lieutenant, Engineer Battalion
Watercolor
Courtesy Frederic Remington Art Museum, Ogdensburg, NY

Aiding a Comrade c. 1890
Oil on canvas, 34 x 48 in.
The Hogg Brothers Collection, Gift of Miss Ima Hogg
Museum of Fine Arts, Houston, TX

The Sun Dance 1890
Oil on canvas, 40 x 27 in.
Courtesy Frederic Remington Art Museum, Ogdensburg, NY

Full Dress Engineer
Watercolor, 34 x 48 in.
Courtesy Frederic Remington Art Museum, Ogdensburg, NY

His Last Stand c. 1890
Oil on canvas, 25¼ x 29¼ in.
Courtesy Sid Richardson Collection of Western Art, Fort Worth, TX

Self Portrait on a Horse c. 1890
Oil on canvas, 29³⁄₁₆ x 19⅝ in.
Courtesy Sid Richardson Collection of Western Art, Fort Worth, TX

A Rural Guard, Mexico c. 1890-92
Watercolor
Peter Newark's Western Americana

In a Stiff Current 1892
Oil (black and white) on canvas, 24 x 36in.
Courtesy Sid Richardson Collection of Western Art, Fort Worth, TX

Right
Bronco Buster c 1895
Oil on canvas
Peter Newark's Western
Americana

Turn Him Loose, Bill c. 1885
Oil on canvas, 25 x 33 in.
Peter Newark's Western Americana/Anschutz Collection

The Blanket Signal 1896
Oil on canvas, 27 x 22 in.
The Hogg Brothers Collection, Gift of Miss Ima Hogg
Museum of Fine Arts, Houston, TX

The Mier Expedition: The Drawing of the Black Bean 1896
Oil on canvas, 20⅛ x 40in.
The Hogg Brothers Collection, Gift of Miss Ima Hogg
Museum of Fine Arts, Houston, TX

Captured 1899
Oil on canvas, 27 x 40⅛ in.
Courtesy Sid Richardson Collection of Western Art, Fort Worth, TX

Charge of the Rough Riders at San Juan Hill 1898
Oil on canvas, 29½ x 50 in.
Courtesy Frederic Remington Art Museum, Ogdensburg, NY

**General French's Irregulars Harassing the Boers
After the Relief of Kimberley** 1900
Oil on canvas
Peter Newark's Military Pictures

Right:
U.S. Infantryman 1901
Peter Newark's Military Pictures

He Rushed the Pony Right to the Barricade c. 1900
Oil on canvas, 27⅛ x 40⅛ in.
Courtesy Sid Richardson Collection of Western Art, Fort Worth, TX

Arizona Cowboy 1901
Peter Newark's Western Americana

Rounded-Up 1901
Oil on canvas, 25 x 48 in.
Courtesy Sid Richardson Collection of Western Art, Fort Worth, TX

Fight for the Waterhole 1901
Oil on canvas, 27¼ x 40⅛ in.
The Hogg Brothers Collection, Gift of Miss Ima Hogg
Museum of Fine Arts, Houston, TX

Cheyenne Brave 1901
Oil on canvas
Peter Newark's Western Americana

Trailing Texas Cattle
Peter Newark's Western Americana

The Winchester
Oil on canvas.
Christie's Images/Bridgeman Art Library, London

A Sioux Chief 1901
Pencil and pastel on composition board, 37⅞ x 22⅞ in.
Courtesy Sid Richardson Collection of Western Art, Fort Worth, TX

Questionable Companionship 1889
Pen and ink on paper, 19¾ x 24⅝ in.
Buffalo Bill Historical Center, Cody, WY./Whitney Purchase Fund

The Emigrants 1904
Oil on canvas, 30 x 45 in.
The Hogg Brothers Collection, Gift of Miss Ima Hogg
Museum of Fine Arts, Houston, TX

Untitled (Dark Green Point on Lake and Reflection in Water)
Oil on board, 9 x 12¼ in.
Buffalo Bill Historical Center, Cody, WY
Gift of The Coe Foundation

Radisson and Groseilliers 1905
Oil on canvas, 18⅛ x 30 in.
Buffalo Bill Historical Center, Cody, WY
Gift of Mrs Karl Frank

Stormy Morning in the Bad Lands 1906
Oil on canvas, 12 x 16 in.
Buffalo Bill Historical Center, Cody, WY
Gift of The Coe Foundation

The Last March 1906
Oil on canvas, 30 x 22 in.
Courtesy Frederic Remington Art Museum, Ogdensburg, NY

A Taint on the Wind 1906
Oil on canvas, 27⅛ x 40 in.
Courtesy Sid Richardson Collection of Western Art, Fort Worth, TX

A Grey Day at Ralph's
Pastel on grey paper, 30 x 22 in.
Courtesy Frederic Remington Art Museum, Ogdensburg, NY

The Last of His Race 1892
Reproduction of a Remington original, painted over by another artist, 18¾ x 13⅞ in.
Courtesy Sid Richardson Collection of Western Art, Fort Worth, TX

Untitled – Early Autumn c. 1907-8
Oil on canvas, 26⅛ x 18⅛ in.
From the Collection of Gilcrease Museum, Tulsa, OK

A Mining Town
Oil on canvas, 27 x 40 in.
Courtesy Frederic Remington Art Museum, Ogdensburg, NY

Scare in a Pack Train 1908
Oil on canvas, 27 x 40 in.
Courtesy Sid Richardson Collection of Western Art, Fort Worth, TX

A Figure of the Night (The Sentinel) 1908
Oil on canvas, 30 x 21⅛ in.
Courtesy Sid Richardson Collection of Western Art, Fort Worth, TX

The Unknown Explorers 1908
Oil on canvas, 30 x 27¼
Courtesy Sid Richardson Collection of Western Art, Fort Worth, TX

Chippewa Bay c. 1907-8
Oil on board, 12 x 16 in
Buffalo Bill Historical Center, Cody, WY
Gift of The Coe Foundation

Apache Medicine Song 1908
Oil on canvas, 27⅛ x 29⅞ in.
Courtesy Sid Richardson Collection of Western Art,
Fort Worth, TX

The Moaning of the Bulls
Oil on canvas, 27 x 40 in.
Courtesy Frederic Remington Art Museum, Ogdensburg, NY

The Luckless Hunter 1909
Oil on canvas, 26⅞ x 28⅞ in.
Courtesy Sid Richardson Collection of Western Art, Fort Worth, TX

Buffalo Runners – Big Horn Basin 1909
Oil on canvas, 30⅛ x 51⅛ in.
Courtesy Sid Richardson Collection of Western Art, Fort Worth, TX

Ghosts of the Past c. 1909
Oil on canvas, 12 x 16 in.
Buffalo Bill Historical Center, Cody, WY
Gift of the Coe Foundation

Night Herder (or The Night Rider)
Oil on board, 12⅛ x18 in.
Buffalo Bill Historical Center, Cody, WY
Gift of The Coe Foundation

Impressionistic Winter Scene
Oil on board, 12 x 18 in.
Buffalo Bill Historical Center, Cody, WY
Gift of The Coe Foundation

Among the Led Horses 1909
Oil on canvas, 27 x 40 in.
Courtesy Sid Richardson Collection of Western Art, Fort Worth, TX

The Snow Trail 1908
Oil on canvas, 27 x 40 in.
Courtesy Frederic Remington Art Museum, Ogdensburg, NY

Hauling in the Gill Net
Oil on canvas, 40 x 27 in.
Courtesy Frederic Remington Art Museum, Ogdensburg, NY

Howl of the Weather 1906
Oil on canvas, 40 x 27 in.
Courtesy Frederic Remington Art Museum, Ogdensburg, NY

Antoine's Cabin c. 1890
Oil on canvas, 28½ x 20in.
Courtesy Frederic Remington Art Museum, Ogdensburg, NY

Boathouse at Ingleneuk 1903
Oil on board, 12 x 18 in.
Courtesy Frederic Remington Art Museum, Ogdensburg, NY

End of the Day 1904
Oil on canvas, 27 x 40 in.
Courtesy Frederic Remington Art Museum, Ogdensburg, NY

Breaking Up the Ice in the Spring 1906
Oil on canvas, 27 x 40in.
Courtesy Frederic Remington Art Museum, Ogdensburg, NY

The Sentinel c. 1907
Oil on canvas, 27 x 36 in.
Courtesy Frederic Remington Art Museum, Ogdensburg, NY

Pete's Shanty 1908
Oil on canvas, 13 x 17 in.
Courtesy Frederic Remington Art Museum, Ogdensburg, NY

Horse Study, Wyoming 1899
Oil on board, 11¾ x 17½ in.
Courtesy Frederic Remington Art Museum, Ogdensburg, NY

The Outlier 1909
Oil on canvas, 30¼ x 27⅛ in.
Courtesy Frederic Remington Art Museum, Ogdensburg, NY

A Study
Oil on canvas.
Courtesy Frederic Remington Art Museum, Ogdensburg, NY

SCULPTURES

The Rattlesnake
Bronze
Peter Newark's Western Americana

The Sergeant
Bronze, 10¼ in. high
Buffalo Bill Historical Center, Cody, WY
Gift of Robert D. Coe

The Cheyenne 1902
Bronze, 20⅛ in. high
Buffalo Bill Historical Center, Cody, WY
Gift of Mrs Henry H.R.Coe

The Outlaw 1903
Bronze, 23½ in. high
Buffalo Bill Historical Center

The Mountain Man 1903
Bronze, 28 in high
Buffalo Bill Historical Center, Cody, WY

Polo 1904
Bronze, 22 in. high
Frederic Remington Art Museum, Ogdensburg, NY

124

The Savage 1908
Bronze, 25 ⅞ in. high
Courtesy Frederic Remington Art Museum,
Ogdensburg, NY

The Broncho Buster 1909
Bronze, 31½ in. high
Buffalo Bill Historical Center, Cody, WY
Gertrude Vanderbilt Whitney Trust Fund

Coming Through the Rye 1902; cast 1907
Bronze, 27½ in. high
Buffalo Bill Historical Center, Cody, WY
Gift of Barbara S.Leggett

ACKNOWLEDGEMENTS

The Author and Publisher gratefully acknowledge the permission granted by the following organisations to publish the illustrations on the following pages:

Frederic Remington Art Museum, Ogdensburg, NY
1, 6, 7, 8, 9, 10, 11, 12, 16, 37, 40, 41, 54/5, 78, 80/1, 84/5, 94, 103, 104/5, 106, 107, 108/9, 110, 111, 112, 113, 114/5, 116, 117, 123, 124

Peter Newark's Military Pictures, Bath
56, 57

Peter Newark's Western Americana, Bath
13, 14, 15, 17, 19, 20, 21, 22 (both), 23, 24, 25, 26/7, 28/9, 36, 45, 47, 48/9, 59, 64/5, 66, 118

Buffalo Bill Historical Center, Cody, WY
18, 32/3, 69, 72/3, 74/5, 76/7, 90/1, 98/9, 100, 101, 119, 120, 121, 122, 125, 126/7

Sid Richardson Collection of Western Art, Fort Worth, TX
30/1, 34, 35, 42/3, 44, 46, 52/3, 58, 60/1, 68, 79, 82, 86/7, 88, 89, 92/3, 95, 96/7, 102

The Museum of Fine Arts, Houston, TX
2, 4, 38/9, 50, 51, 62/3, 70/1

The Thomas Gilcrease Institute of American History and Art Tulsa, OK.
83
Bridgeman Art Library, London
67